Everyday Mathematics

Everything Math Deck
Activities

 Wright Group

The **McGraw·Hill** Companies

McGraw Hill Wright Group

Copyright © 2004 by Wright Group/McGraw-Hill.

All rights reserved. Permission is granted to reproduce the material contained herin on the condition that such material be reproduced only for classroom use; be provided to students, teachers, or families without charge; and be used solely in conjunction with *Everyday Mathematics*. Any other reproduction, for use or sale, is prohibited without the prior written permission from the publisher.

Printed in the United States of America.

Send all inquiries to:
Wright Group/McGraw-Hill
P.O. Box 812960
Chicago, IL 60681

ISBN 0-07-600260-8

7 8 9 10 11 12 PBM 09 08 07 06 05

Contents

Introduction	1
Description of Card Decks	2
Using Card Deck Activities in the Classroom	3
Setting Up an Activities Corner	5
Using the Everything Math Deck with *Everyday Mathematics*	6
Activities and Games by Strand	7
Using the Everything Math Deck with *Everyday Mathematics* (chart)	8
Activities and Games by Strand (chart)	17
Directions for Activities and Games	25
Addition Top-It	26
Almost One	27
Arrays	28
Before and After	29

Between	30
Challenge with Signed Numbers	31
Choose the Operation	32
Composite Number Challenge	33
Composite Numbers Memory Game	34
Different Name, Same Value	35
Dot Addition	36
Drawing Polygons	37
Drawing Triangular Numbers	38
Equivalent Fractions	39
First to 23	40
Fraction Concentration	41
Fraction Flash	42
Fraction Number Line	43
Fraction Quotient	44
Fraction Sum	45
Fraction Top-It	46
Fractions Small and Large	47
Free Play	48
Going Fishing	49
Greater Than	50
Integer Number Line	51

Contents

Lucky Nine	52
Match It	53
Matching Numbers with Counters	54
Math Game	55
Missing Addends	56
Mixed Numbers	57
Multiplication Top-It	58
Name That Number	59
Naming Figures	61
Number Guess	62
Number Line Game	63
Number Sentence Contest	64
Numbers and Dot Patterns I	65
Numbers and Dot Patterns II	66
Odd and Even Numbers	67
Ordering a Set of Fractions	68
Ordering Fractions with Same Denominator	69
Ordering Numbers	70
Polygons	71
Polygons Alike and Different	72
Prime and Composite Facts	73
Prime or Composite?	74
Primes and Composites	75
Product Game	76
Product Production	77
Rectangular Arrays	78
Smallest to Largest	79
Sorting the Deck	80
Square Numbers	81
Steps	82
Sums	83
Top-It	84
Top-It with Integers	85
Triangular Numbers	87
Triple Challenge	88
Unit Fractions	89
Writing 1 as a Fraction	90

Introduction

Welcome to the new *Everyday Mathematics*® card deck activity books!

- *Everything Math Deck Activities*
- *Fraction/Decimal/Percent Deck Activities*
- *Time Deck Activities*
- *Money Deck Activities*

These card deck activity books provide an enjoyable way for students to practice and master basic math skills, without the use of routine drill and daily worksheets. The activities and games engage students' interest as they develop their ability to think critically and solve problems.

These activity books provide teachers with information and suggestions on using the card decks with the *Everyday Mathematics* program. They also include new, supplemental activities and games for remediation or enrichment and can be readily used in the classroom, activity centers, or at home. In particular, resource teachers will find the card decks and activity books to be useful tools for individualizing instruction and providing additional reinforcement of math concepts taught in the classroom.

Everything Math Deck

Fraction/Decimal/Percent Deck

2 Description of Card Decks

Description of Card Decks

Money Card Deck

Time Card Deck

Each card deck contains a set of durable, laminated cards. They can be used with the *Everyday Mathematics* card deck activity books or the *Everyday Mathematics* Games Kit.

Money Deck

Money cards show pictures of various combinations of pennies, nickels, dimes, and quarters.

Time Deck

Time cards show digital clock times, analog clock times, and times written in words for 18 different times.

Fraction/Decimal/Percent Deck

These cards show 18 different fractions, decimals, and percents. The fractions, decimals, and percents are equivalent to each other.

Everything Math Deck

This two-sided card deck is used throughout *Everyday Mathematics*. On one side, the cards show a number deck with 4 cards for each of the numbers 0 through 10, and 1 card for numbers 11 through 20. Numbers are printed in blue or black to easily represent positive and negative numbers. The reverse sides of number cards 1–10 show fractions represented in a variety of ways.

Using Card Deck Activities in the Classroom

Each card deck activity book contains the following:

- Table showing how the card decks can be used with individual lessons in the *Everyday Mathematics* core program.

- Table listing the new activities and games by content strand. It also identifies the appropriate grade levels and skill being reinforced by each activity or game.

- Over 40 new activities for each card deck. The activities are primarily for small groups, partnerships, or individual use. They may be used by the classroom teacher or by a resource teacher or an adult aide/volunteer to provide additional remediation or enrichment for students outside of the classroom.

- The object of each activity, the appropriate number of students, and any additional materials needed are included on each activity page.

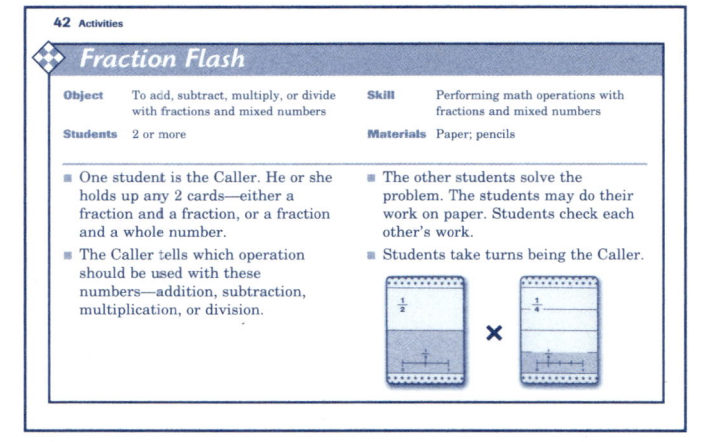

Using Card Deck Activities in the Classroom (cont.)

The card deck activities can be organized and implemented in your classroom in many ways. Here are some ideas to consider as you customize the use of these activities for your students:

- Use the Activities and Games by Strand chart to find the activity you need for those students who require additional practice with a skill or concept.

- Choose individuals who work well together in groups.

- Most activities require 10–15 minutes and do not have to be done during math time.

- Make copies of several activities, particularly those that reinforce the math concept(s) you are currently teaching or have covered in class, and allow students to choose which one to do during a free period or indoor recess.

- At Grades K–2, you may want to read the directions aloud to students or select a capable student to read the directions to a small group.

Sending Activities Home

The card deck activities and games provide an excellent way for students to practice concepts or skills at home. Other students will benefit from doing the activities as enrichment. To create your own home activity kits, place a copy of the activity and all the materials needed for the activity in a resealable plastic bag. Make a sign-out sheet to keep track of the activities being sent home.

Setting Up an Activities Corner

You may want to set up an Activities Corner in your classroom—some place where individual students or small groups of students can work on the card deck activities or games. Set up 3 to 5 activity stations with copies of activities and all the materials, if any, needed for the activities. Rotate the activities according to the concepts or skills that require additional practice or enrichment.

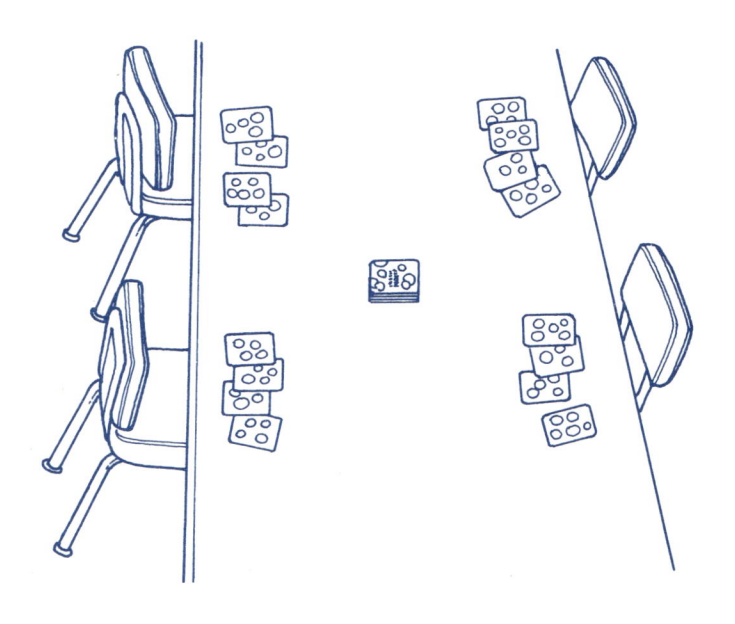

Using the Everything Math Deck with *Everyday Mathematics*

The chart on pages 8–16 identifies all of the lessons in the *Teacher's Lesson Guides* for which the Everything Math Deck can be used. The table is organized by grade level. It identifies the page number, the lesson number, and the name of the activity within the lesson for which you may use the Everything Math Deck. (For Kindergarten the strand is indicated instead of the lesson number.)

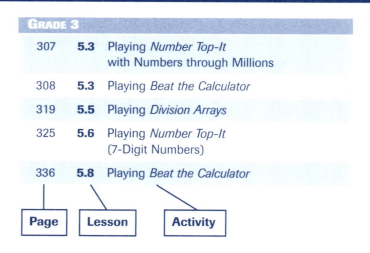

Activities and Games by Strand

The *Everyday Mathematics* curriculum is divided into the following strands:

- Numeration
- Operations & Computation
- Patterns, Functions, & Algebra
- Geometry
- Measurement & Reference Frames, which includes measurement, clocks, and money
- Data & Chance

The chart on pages 17–24 lists all of the card deck activities and games that work on developing skills and concepts for a particular strand. Some activities or games appear in more than one strand. The activities and games are listed in alphabetical order within each strand. The appropriate grade level(s) are given for each activity or game. The range of grade levels is broad, allowing for the fact that the activity or game may be used for remediation and/or enrichment across several grade levels. The skill covered by each activity or game and the page number on which the directions can be found are included.

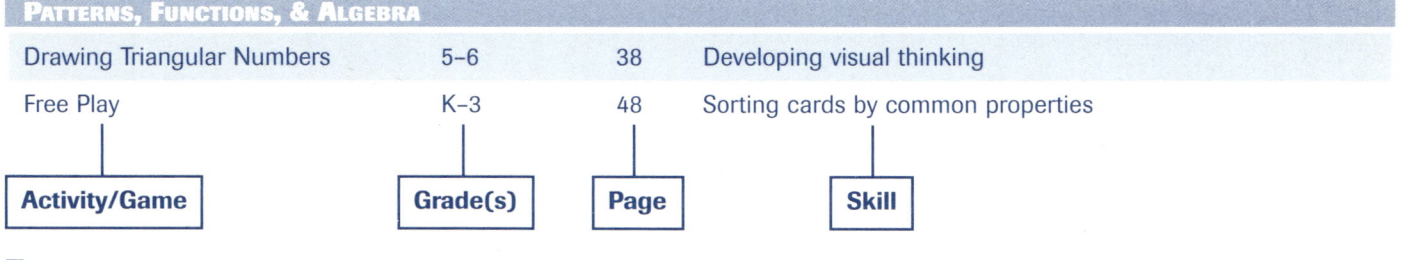

PATTERNS, FUNCTIONS, & ALGEBRA			
Drawing Triangular Numbers	5–6	38	Developing visual thinking
Free Play	K–3	48	Sorting cards by common properties

Activity/Game Grade(s) Page Skill

Using the Everything Math Deck with *Everyday Mathematics*

KINDERGARTEN

Page	Strand	Activity
89	Numeration	Concentration with Number Cards and Dominoes
115	Numeration	Slate-Writing Activities
116	Numeration	Listen and Do (10–20)
169	Numeration	Classroom Playing Cards
170	Numeration	Top-It
202	Operations	Operator, Operator
226	Operations	Domino Name Collections
278	Operations	"What Number Am I Thinking Of?"
289	Numeration	Ascending and Descending Order

Using the Everything Math Deck with *Everyday Mathematics*

GRADE 1

Page	Lesson	Activity
36	1.6	Introducing *Top-It*
53	1.10	Playing *Top-It* in Small Groups
58	1.11	Playing *Top-It*
91	2.1	Playing *Top-It*
143	2.12	Playing *Who Am I Thinking Of?*
170	3.1	Playing *Before and After*
289	4.7	Sorting Dominoes by the Total Number of Dots
347	5.3	Playing *Top-It* with Relation Symbols
367	5.7	Playing the *Difference Game*
489	6.1	Introducing *Addition Top-It*
495	6.2	Playing *Addition Top-It*
502	6.3	Playing the *Difference Game*
511	6.5	Playing *Addition Top-It*

Page	Lesson	Activity
521	6.7	Playing Math Games: *Addition Top-It*
547	6.12	Playing *Addition Top-It*
573	7.2	Playing an Addition Fact Game: *Addition Top-It*
651	8.8	Playing *Addition Top-It*
677	9.1	Using the Number Cards to Make the Largest and Smallest Numbers
746	10.5	Finding Combinations of Digits

9 Using the Everything Math Deck

Using the Everything Math Deck

Using the Everything Math Deck with *Everyday Mathematics*

Grade 2

Page	Lesson	Activity
33	1.4	Demonstrating and Playing *Addition Top-It*
38	1.5	Playing *Addition Top-It*
42	1.6	Playing *Addition Top-It*
51	1.8	Playing *Addition Top-It*
68	1.12	Playing *Addition Top-It*
69	1.12	Playing *Digit Discovery*
73	1.13	Exploration C: Sorting Dominoes
78	1.14	Play *Digit Discovery*
99	2.2	Playing *Addition Top-It*
130	2.9	Demonstrating *Name That Number*, Playing *Name That Number*
136	2.10	Playing *Name That Number*
170	3.1	Matching Numbers and Displays of Base-10 Blocks
176	3.2	Playing the *Digit Game*
184	3.4	Exploration A: Building and Renaming Numbers
259	4.7	Exploration E: Tiling Surfaces with Different Shapes
268	4.8	Reviewing Place-Value Concepts
357	6.1	Playing *Three Addends*
364	6.2	Playing *Addition Top-It*
383	6.5	Building and Renaming Numbers
393	6.7	Playing *Three Addends*
420	6.12	Play *Three Addends*
532	7.4	Playing *Three Addends*
597	8.4	Playing *Name That Number*
746	10.10	Playing a Variation of the *Digit Game*
799	11.5	Playing *Multiplication Draw*
856	12.5	Playing *Addition Card Draw*

Using the Everything Math Deck with *Everyday Mathematics*

GRADE 3

Page	Lesson	Activity
28	1.3	Looking up Information in the *Student Reference Book*
33	1.4	Playing *Addition Top-It*
39	1.5	Reviewing Place-Value Concepts
42	1.6	Playing *Name That Number*
52	1.8	Playing *Beat the Calculator*
58	1.9	Playing *Name That Number*
74	1.12	Playing Games to Practice the Addition Facts
79	1.13	Play *Name That Number*
80	1.13	Play *Beat the Calculator*
103	2.2	Playing *Name That Number* Using Multiples of 10
145	2.9	Playing *Three Addends*
150	2.10	Play *Name That Number* Using Multiples of 10; Play *Three Addends*

Page	Lesson	Activity
196	3.6	Practicing Basic Facts
211	3.9	Play *Three Addends*
240	4.3	Playing *Division Arrays*
245	4.4	Playing *Division Arrays*
250	4.5	Playing *Beat the Calculator*
257	4.6	Playing *Beat the Calculator*
278	4.10	Play *Division Arrays*; Play *Beat the Calculator*
300	5.2	Playing *Number Top-It* (5-Digit Numbers)
307	5.3	Playing *Number Top-It* with Numbers through Millions
308	5.3	Playing *Beat the Calculator*
319	5.5	Playing *Division Arrays*
325	5.6	Playing *Number Top-It* (7-Digit Numbers)

11 Using the Everything Math Deck

Using the Everything Math Deck with *Everyday Mathematics*

GRADE 3 (CONT.)

Page	Lesson	Activity	Page	Lesson	Activity
336	5.8	Playing *Beat the Calculator*	582	7.10	Play the Extended Facts Version of *Beat the Calculator*
342	5.9	Playing *Division Arrays*	607	8.2	Practicing Multiplication Facts
348	5.10	Playing *Number Top-It* (3-Place Decimals)	682	9.6	Introducing *Factor Bingo*
382	6.1	Playing *Number Top-It* (3-Place Decimals)	683	9.6	Playing *Factor Bingo*
			684	9.6	Playing *Array Bingo*
416	6.7	Playing *Beat the Calculator*	689	9.7	Sharing Money
546	7.3	Play *Multiplication Bingo*	729	9.14	Play *Factor Bingo*
548	7.3	Playing the Advanced Version of *Multiplication Bingo*			
557	7.5	Playing a Class "Basketball" Game			
562	7.6	Playing *Beat the Calculator* with Extended Facts			
566	7.7	Solving Problems by Estimation			
577	7.9	Playing the Decimal Version of *Number Top-It*			

Using the Everything Math Deck with *Everyday Mathematics*

GRADE 4

Page	Lesson	Activity
84	2.2	Playing *Name That Number*
86	2.2	Playing *Name That Number* with Multiples of 10
97	2.4	Playing *Number Top-It*
101	2.5	Playing *Addition Top-It*
107	2.6	Playing *Subtraction Top-It*
113	2.7	Playing *Name That Number* and *High-Toss Number*
125	2.9	Playing *Subtraction Target Practice*
131	2.10	Play *Name That Number*
161	3.3	Practicing Multiplication Facts
188	3.9	Playing *Name That Number*
222	4.2	Playing *Number Top-It* (Decimals)
241	4.6	Playing *Number Top-It* (Decimals)
283	5.1	Playing *Beat the Calculator*

Page	Lesson	Activity
287	5.2	Playing *Multiplication Wrestling*
344	5.11	Playing *High-Number Toss* or *Number Top-It*
760	10.6	Playing the *Credits/Debits Game*
798	11.3	Playing the *Credits/Debits Game*
810	11.5	Playing the *Credits/Debits Game*
816	11.6	Playing the *Credits/Debits Game* (Advanced Version)

13 Using the Everything Math Deck

Using the Everything Math Deck with *Everyday Mathematics*

Grade 5

Page	Lesson	Activity	Page	Lesson	Activity
25	1.3	Playing Fact-Skills Games to Practice Multiplication Facts	113	2.7	Playing *Beat the Calculator* with Extended Facts
30	1.4	Practicing Multiplication Facts through Games	129	2.10	Playing *Number Top-It*
40	1.6	Practicing Multiplication Facts through Games	133	2.11	Play *Subtraction Target Practice*; Play *Number Top-It*
44	1.7	Playing *Factor Top-It*	285	5.4	Making Equivalent Fractions
55	1.9	Playing *Name That Number*; Playing *Factor Bingo*	309	5.8	Playing *2-4-5-10 Frac-Tac-Toe* (Percent Version)
60	1.10	Play *Beat the Calculator*	325	5.11	Playing Bingo Versions of *2-4-5-10 Frac-Tac-Toe*
77	2.1	Playing Games Using Multiplication Facts	335	5.13	Play *2-4-5-10 Frac-Tac-Toe*
91	2.3	Playing *Addition Top-It*; Playing *Subtraction Target Practice*	359	6.2	Explaining the Challenge Questions for *First to 21*
96	2.4	Playing *High-Number Toss*	366	6.3	Playing *First to 21*
112	2.7	Playing *Multiplication Bull's-Eye*	391	6.8	Playing *Frac-Tac-Toe*

Using the Everything Math Deck with *Everyday Mathematics*

GRADE 5 (CONT.)

Page	Lesson	Activity
534	7.6	Playing *Name That Number*
540	7.7	Playing *Top-It*
546	7.8	Playing *High-Number Toss*
563	7.11	Play *Name That Number*
615	8.6	Playing *Fraction Multiplication Top-It*
619	8.7	Playing *Name That Number*
624	8.8	Playing *Frac-Tac-Toe*
654	8.13	Play *Frac-Tac-Toe*
694	9.5	Playing *Frac-Tac-Toe*
846	11.6	Playing *Name That Number*
880	12.2	Playing *Frac-Tac-Toe*
891	12.4	Playing *Name That Number*

Using the Everything Math Deck with *Everyday Mathematics*

Grade 6

Page	Lesson	Activity	Page	Lesson	Activity
31	1.4	Playing *Landmark Shark*	583	7.8	Playing *Name That Number*
35	1.5	Playing *Landmark Shark*	635	8.6	Math Message Follow-Up
55	1.9	Playing *Landmark Shark*	640	8.6	Solving Challenging Ratio Problems
102	2.4	Playing *Doggone Decimal*	702	9.1	Playing *Name That Number*
257	4.8	Playing *Frac-Tac-Toe*	703	9.1	Playing *Multiplication Wrestling*
469	6.3	Playing the Advanced Version of *Credits/Debits Game*			
473	6.4	Playing *Top-It* Games with Positive and Negative Numbers			
497	6.8	Playing *Name That Number*			
520	6.12	Playing *Solution Search*			
547	7.2	Generating Random Numbers			
558	7.4	Simulating Results with a Tree Diagram			
559	7.4	Playing *Frac-Tac-Toe*			
578	7.7	Creating a Fair Game			

Activities and Games by Strand

NUMERATION

Activity/Game	Grade(s)	Page	Skill
Almost One	4–6	27	Ordering and estimating with fractions
Before and After	K–2	29	Identifying numbers that are 1 more or 1 less than a given number
Between	4–6	30	Ordering positive and negative numbers
Challenge with Signed Numbers	5–6	31	Comparing positive and negative numbers
Composite Number Challenge	5–6	33	Recognizing primes and composites
Composite Numbers Memory Game	5–6	34	Recognizing composite numbers
Different Name, Same Value	2–6	35	Discovering equivalent fractions
Equivalent Fractions	2–6	39	Recognizing equivalent fractions pictorially
Fraction Number Line	2–6	43	Recognizing the meaning of fractions
Fraction Top-It	1–6	46	Comparing fractions
Fractions Small and Large	4–6	47	Ordering fractions
Going Fishing	5–6	49	Recognizing equivalent fractions

Activities and Games by Strand

NUMERATION (CONT.)

Activity/Game	Grade(s)	Page	Skill
Greater Than	4–6	50	Understanding place value; comparing whole numbers
Matching Numbers with Counters	K–2	54	Connecting concrete representations to numerals
Math Game	4–6	55	Understanding number theory, fractions, and operations
Mixed Numbers	2–6	57	Recognizing the meaning of mixed numbers
Number Line Game	4–6	63	Understanding the meaning of positive and negative numbers
Odd and Even Numbers	2–3	67	Counting by 2s
Ordering a Set of Fractions	4–6	68	Ordering fractions
Ordering Fractions with Same Denominator	1–6	69	Understanding fractions
Ordering Numbers	1–3	70	Counting forward and backward
Prime and Composite Facts	5–6	73	Identifying factors
Prime or Composite?	2–3	74	Discovering properties of prime and composite numbers between 2 and 9
Primes and Composites	5–6	75	Discovering properties of prime and composite numbers between 11 and 20

Activities and Games by Strand

NUMERATION (CONT.)

Activity/Game	Grade(s)	Page	Skill
Rectangular Arrays	5–6	78	Classifying numbers
Smallest to Largest	4–6	79	Understanding place value
Steps	K–2	82	Recognizing number values
Top-It	1–3	84	Comparing whole numbers
Unit Fractions	K–6	89	Recognizing the parts and meaning of fractions
Writing 1 as a Fraction	1–6	90	Finding equivalent names for numbers

Activities and Games by Strand

OPERATIONS & COMPUTATION

Activity/Game	Grade(s)	Page	Skill
Addition Top-It	1–3	26	Adding whole numbers mentally
Arrays	2–3	28	Understanding the meaning of multiplication
Choose the Operation	2–3	32	Adding, subtracting, and multiplying mentally
Dot Addition	K–2	36	Adding with the aid of pictures
First to 23	1–3	40	Adding whole numbers
Fraction Concentration	4–6	41	Multiplying fractions
Fraction Flash	4–6	42	Performing math operations with fractions and mixed numbers
Fraction Quotient	5–6	44	Dividing and adding fractions
Fraction Sum	4–6	45	Adding fractions
Match It	3–6	53	Using equivalent names for numbers
Multiplication Top-It	4–6	58	Practicing multiplication facts
Name That Number	2–6	59	Using equivalent names for numbers
Number Guess	K–3	62	Understanding the meaning of addition, subtraction, and multiplication

Activities and Games by Strand

OPERATIONS & COMPUTATION (CONT.)

Activity/Game	Grade(s)	Page	Skill
Product Game	4–6	76	Multiplying fractions
Product Production	4–6	77	Multiplying a 2-digit number by a 1-digit number
Sums	4–5	83	Understanding place value and adding 4-digit numbers

Activities and Games by Strand

GEOMETRY

Activity/Game	Grade(s)	Page	Skill
Drawing Polygons	K–6	37	Drawing and identifying polygons
Naming Figures	2–6	61	Identifying figures by numbers of sides
Polygons	2–6	71	Recognizing and naming polygons
Polygons Alike and Different	K–6	72	Identifying properties of geometric figures
Sorting the Deck	2–5	80	Recognizing shapes

Activities and Games by Strand

PATTERNS, FUNCTIONS, & ALGEBRA

Activity/Game	Grade(s)	Page	Skill
Drawing Triangular Numbers	5–6	38	Developing visual thinking
Free Play	K–3	48	Sorting cards by common properties
Integer Number Line	5–6	51	Comparing positive and negative numbers
Lucky Nine	5–6	52	Understanding the order of operations
Missing Addends	2–3	56	Thinking algebraically
Number Sentence Contest	4–6	64	Writing number sentences for a given value
Numbers and Dot Patterns I	K–2	65	Connecting numerals with pictorial representations
Numbers and Dot Patterns II	1–3	66	Classifying according to established criteria
Sorting the Deck	2–5	80	Recognizing shapes
Square Numbers	4–6	81	Developing visual thinking
Top-It with Integers	4–6	85	Adding and subtracting integers

Activities and Games by Strand

Patterns, Functions, & Algebra (cont.)

Activity/Game	Grade(s)	Page	Skill
Triangular Numbers	2–3	87	Developing visual thinking
Triple Challenge	5–6	88	Writing expressions to make the smallest whole number possible

Directions for Activities and Games

The following activities and games were designed so that students could read and do them on their own. For some students, however, you may want to read the directions aloud or select a capable student to read the directions aloud to a small group.

Each activity or game lists the object, the skill being practiced, the number of students who can play, and any additional materials needed.

Most of the activities and games require just one Everything Math Deck. Other activities may require the use of one or more of the following items: paper; pencils; crayons; counters; removable stickers; and index cards.

You may want to read the games and activities ahead of time to determine if your students will need any assistance.

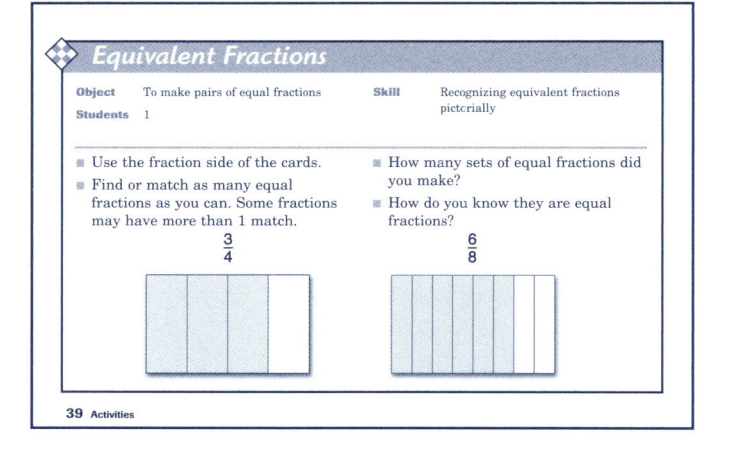

Addition Top-It

Object To collect the most cards
Students 2 to 4

Skill Adding whole numbers mentally

- The Dealer mixes the cards and places them number-side down in a pile.
- Each student turns over 2 cards and calls out the sum of the numbers.
- The student with the greatest sum wins the round and takes all the cards.
- In case of a tie, each tied student turns over 2 more cards and calls out the sum. The student with the greatest sum takes all the cards from both plays.
- The game ends when there are not enough cards left for each student to have another turn. The student who has the most cards wins.

Try This

- Use only the number cards 0–10.

 **Almost One**

Object To order fractions from smallest to largest

Skill Ordering and estimating with fractions

Students 1 or more

Materials Paper; pencils

- Take the following fraction cards from the deck: $\frac{7}{8}$, $\frac{4}{5}$, $\frac{3}{4}$, $\frac{5}{6}$, and $\frac{2}{3}$.

- Put the cards in order from smallest to largest. You may use the blue shading on the cards to help you.

- Study the cards. What whole number are all these fractions closest to?

- Use estimation to find the sum of all the fractions, to the nearest whole number.

27 Activities

Arrays

Object To form arrays with sets of 2
Students 1 or more

Skill Understanding the meaning of multiplication
Materials 10 counters

- Take all the cards that have dots arranged in lines, squares, or rectangles.
- Look at the cards for 2, 4, 6, 8, and 10. How many sets of 2 are in each number?
- Turn the cards sideways. How many sets of 2 are in each number?
- Use counters to make each array shown on the cards.
- As you make each array, describe the array in words. For example, "When I have 4 sets of 2, I can say 4 times 2 equals 8."
- You can also describe each array in terms of addition. For example, "2 plus 2 plus 2 equals 6."

 # Before and After

Object To have fewer cards than the other player

Students 2

Skill Identifying numbers that are 1 more or 1 less than a given number

Materials All 0–10 cards from 1 deck

- The Dealer mixes the cards and gives 6 cards, one at a time, to each student. The Dealer puts the rest of the cards facedown in a pile.

- Each student places 2 cards side by side and faceup in front of himself or herself. Each student holds the remaining 4 cards in his or her hand.

- Students take turns.

- A student looks for any number in his or her hand that is 1 more or 1 less than any of the 4 faceup numbers. The student puts the card on top of the faceup number. The student takes a new card from the pile.

- If a student can't place any cards, he or she loses a turn.

- The game is over when there are no more cards left in the pile or when no student can place any more cards.

29 Activities

Between

Object To have the least number of cards at the end of the game

Students 2 to 4

Skill Ordering positive and negative numbers

Materials All 0–10 cards from 1 deck

- The Dealer picks 1 blue card and 1 black card from the deck.
- The Dealer places the blue card and black card on the table to form the 2 ends of a number line. The blue cards are negative and the black cards are positive.
- The Dealer shuffles the rest of the cards and gives 10 cards to each student.
- Students take turns trying to place cards. To place a card, its number must be between the 2 numbers that form the ends of the number line. If a student has a card that matches a card already on the table, he or she can put it on top of that card.
- The game is over when no student can place any more cards.
- The student with the least number of cards left over wins.

Challenge with Signed Numbers

Object   To collect the most cards at the end of the game

Students 2 to 4

Skill   Comparing positive and negative numbers

- The Dealer shuffles the deck and divides the cards evenly between the students. Students place the cards number-side down in front of them.

- The black numbers are positive. The blue numbers are negative. Zero is neither positive nor negative, so the black zero and blue zero are the same.

- Each student turns over the top card of his or her pile. The student with the greatest number wins all 4 cards.

- In case of a tie, each tied student turns over a second card. The student with the greatest number takes all cards from both plays.

- The game is over when all the cards have been taken. The student with the most cards wins the game.

Try This

- At the end of the game, each student adds the numbers on his or her cards. The student with the greatest total wins the game.

31 Activities

Choose the Operation

Object	To find the sum, difference, or product	**Skill**	Adding, subtracting, and multiplying mentally
Students	2	**Materials**	Cards 0–10, 1–20, 11–20, or the whole deck

- Students take out the cards they wish to use. The other cards are set aside.
- One student is the Dealer and one is the Solver.
- The Dealer takes 2 cards from the top of the deck and shows them to the Solver. The Dealer states which operation (addition, subtraction, or multiplication) he or she wants the Solver to use.
- The Solver does the operation with the 2 numbers. The Dealer checks the answer.
- Students take turns being the Dealer and the Solver.

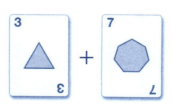
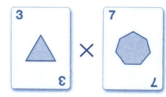

Composite Number Challenge

Object   To collect more cards

Students   2

Skill   Recognizing primes and composites

Materials   All 0–10 cards from 1 deck (or use the whole deck)

- The Dealer shuffles the deck and divides the cards evenly between the students, number-side down.

- Each student turns over the top card of his or her pile. The student with a composite number wins both cards. If neither number is composite, the student with the greater number card wins both cards.

- If both cards are composite, the student with the greater number takes both cards.

- If both cards are the same number, each student turns over a second card. The student with a composite number takes all 4 cards.

- The game is over when all the cards have been taken. The student with more cards wins.

Try This

- At the end of the game, each student adds the numbers on his or her cards. The student with the greater total wins.

33 Activities

Composite Numbers Memory Game

Object To collect more cards at the end of the game

Students 2

Skill Recognizing composite numbers

Materials All 1–10 cards from 1 deck

- The Dealer shuffles the deck and places all the cards number-side down in a 5-by-8 array.
- Students take turns turning over 2 cards. If the sum of the 2 cards is a composite number, the student keeps the 2 cards. If not, the student returns the cards to their original positions.
- Play continues until all the cards have been taken. The student with more cards wins.

Try This

- Use an operation other than addition. The result can be prime, divisible by 3, even, odd, and so on.

Different Name, Same Value

Object To find all the fraction cards equivalent to $\frac{1}{2}$

Students 1 or more

Skill Discovering equivalent fractions

Materials Paper; pencils

- Find all the fraction cards in which half the parts are shaded blue.

- Make sure the blue shaded parts are equal on all of these cards.

- Which point is labeled on each number line? Compare this to the amount shaded on the card.

- Write down all the fractions shown on the cards. What do all these fractions equal?

Take the Challenge

- Try to find fraction cards that are equivalent to $\frac{1}{4}$ and $\frac{3}{4}$.

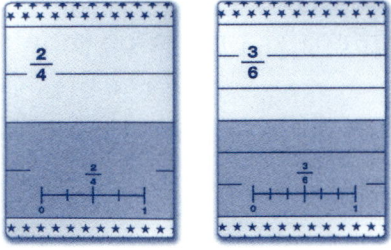

Both cards have the same value.

35 Activities

Dot Addition

Object To practice basic addition facts
Students 1 or more

Skill Adding with the aid of pictures
Materials Paper; pencils; removable stickers (for Try This)

- Find all the cards that show dots on them. Set the other cards aside.
- Mix the cards with dots and place them number-side down in a pile.
- Take the top 2 cards from the pile and add them. You can either count the dots or write the problem on a piece of paper.

Try This

- Draw dots on the 11 through 20 cards and add them to the playing deck (or use removable round labels or stickers).

Drawing Polygons

Object   To draw polygons with different numbers of sides

Students   1

Skill   Drawing and identifying polygons

Materials   Paper; pencil or crayons

- Find all the cards that show polygons.
- Draw each polygon.
- Write the name of each polygon below your picture.
- Keep your pictures in a folder. Try drawing these shapes again at a later time. Compare them with the first set you drew. Do they look better?

Try This

- For each polygon, draw an object from the classroom that has that shape. Or, write the name of that object.

Drawing Triangular Numbers

Object To draw triangular numbers
Students 1
Skill Developing visual thinking
Materials Paper; pencil

- Find all the cards that show dots that form a triangle. What kinds of triangles are they?
- Triangular numbers can also be drawn as right triangles. For example:

```
3         6          10
•         •          •
• •       • •        • •
          • • •      • • •
                     • • • •
```

- Draw right-triangular arrangements for 15 and 21.

Take the Challenge

- What must be added to each of these right-triangular numbers to make a square number?

Equivalent Fractions

Object   To make pairs of equal fractions

Students   1

Skill   Recognizing equivalent fractions pictorially

- Use the fraction side of the cards.
- Find or match as many equal fractions as you can. Some fractions may have more than 1 match.

- How many sets of equal fractions did you make?
- How do you know they are equal fractions?

$\dfrac{3}{4}$

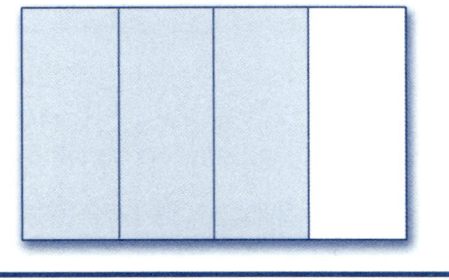

$\dfrac{6}{8}$

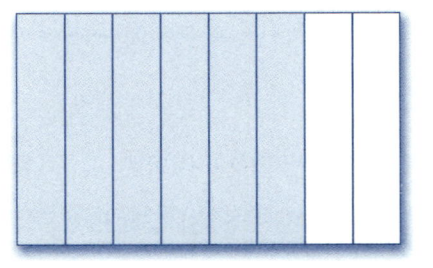

39 Activities

First to 23

Object To get as close to 23 without going over

Students 3 to 4

Skill Adding whole numbers

- One student is the Dealer. The Dealer mixes the cards and gives 2 cards to each of the other students.
- Each student finds the sum of his or her cards. Each student may ask the Dealer for more cards, one at a time, to try to reach a total of 23.
- The student who gets a sum closest to 23, without going over, is the winner and becomes the Dealer.

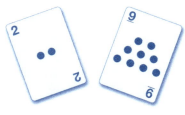

$2 + 9 = 11$
$2 + 9 + 8 = 19$
Close enough to 23?

Fraction Concentration

Object   To collect more cards at the end of the game

Students   2

Skill   Multiplying fractions

Materials   All fraction cards from 1 deck

- One student shuffles the deck and arranges the cards fraction-side down in a 6-by-7 array.

- Students take turns turning over 2 cards at a time. The student multiplies the fractions on the cards.

- If the product of the 2 fractions is greater than $\frac{1}{2}$, the student keeps both cards.

- If the product of the 2 cards is less than $\frac{1}{2}$, the student returns the cards fraction-side down.

- The game lasts for 10 minutes, or until all or most of the cards have been taken. The student with more cards wins.

Try This

- Instead of multiplying, students add the 2 fractions. Students take the cards if their sum is greater than 1.

Fraction Flash

Object To add, subtract, multiply, or divide with fractions and mixed numbers

Students 2 or more

Skill Performing math operations with fractions and mixed numbers

Materials Paper; pencils

- One student is the Caller. He or she holds up any 2 cards—either a fraction and a fraction, or a fraction and a whole number.
- The Caller tells which operation should be used with these numbers—addition, subtraction, multiplication, or division.
- The other students solve the problem. The students may do their work on paper. Students check each other's work.
- Students take turns being the Caller.

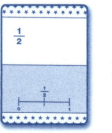 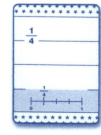

Fraction Number Line

Object   To plot fractions on a number line

Students   2 or more

Skill   Recognizing the meaning of fractions

Materials   Paper; pencils

- One student draws a number line on the paper. It should be marked 0 at one end and 1 at the other end.

- Students take turns picking a fraction card from the deck and writing the fraction on the number line. They may use the number line on the card to help them decide where the fraction should be placed.

- Think about this question: Are the points you drew on the number line exact, or are they estimates?

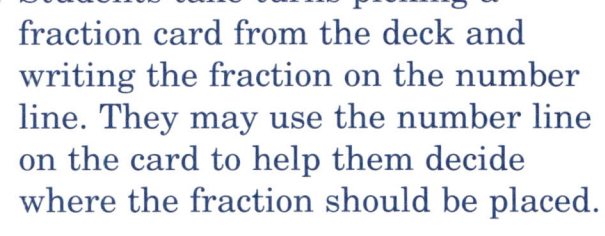

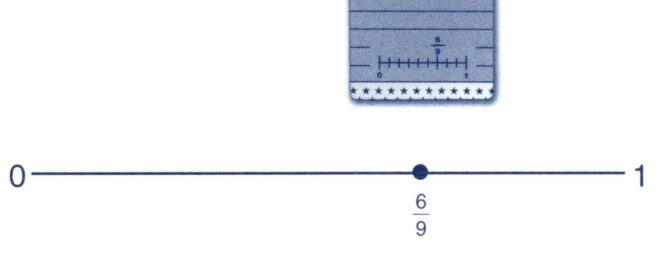

43 Activities

Fraction Quotient

Object   To get the greater score
Students 2

Skill   Dividing and adding fractions
Materials All fraction cards from 1 deck; paper; pencils

- One student shuffles the deck and places it fraction-side down on the table.
- Each student takes 2 cards and turns them over.
- Students choose one card to be the dividend and the other to be the divisor.
- Students divide their fractions. The student with the greater quotient wins $\frac{1}{2}$ point.
- Play continues until there are no more cards in the deck. The student with the greater total score wins.

Try This

- The score for each round can be any fraction, such as $\frac{3}{4}$ point or $1\frac{1}{2}$ points.
- The game can be played by finding products instead of quotients.

Fraction Sum

Object   To collect more cards

Students   2

Skill   Adding fractions

Materials   All fraction cards from 1 deck

- One student shuffles the deck and gives 10 cards to each student. Students place their cards fraction-side down.

- Each student turns over 2 cards and adds the fractions on the cards. The student with the greater sum takes all 4 cards.

- If there is a tie, each student turns over 2 more cards. The student with the higher sum takes all 8 cards.

- The game is over when all cards have been played. The student with more cards wins.

Try This

- Play the game with subtraction. The student with the greater difference wins each round.

45 Activities

Fraction Top-It

Object To collect more cards
Students 2

Skill Comparing fractions
Materials All fraction cards from 1 deck

- One student shuffles the cards and places them fraction-side down in a pile.
- Each student turns over a card from the top of the deck.
- The students compare the fractions using the shaded parts of the cards. The student with the larger fraction takes both cards.

- If there is a tie, then each student turns over another card. The student with the larger fraction takes all 4 cards.
- The game is over when all cards have been played. The student with more cards wins.

Fractions Small and Large

Object   To order fractions from smallest to largest

Students   1

Skill   Ordering fractions

Materials   Paper; pencil

- Pick any 10 fraction cards from the deck.
- Put the cards in order from the smallest to the largest fraction. Use the blue shading on the cards to help you.
- On your paper, write the fractions in order from smallest to largest.

47 Activities

48 Activities

Free Play

Object   To sort the cards by attributes   **Skill**   Sorting cards by common properties
Students   1

- Look at all the cards.
- Find cards that show fractions. Place them in a pile.
- Find cards that show different shapes. Place them in a pile.
- See if you can find other cards that have something in common.

A shape card

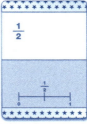
A fraction card

# Going Fishing

Object   To be the first student to run out of cards

Students   2 to 4

Skill   Recognizing equivalent fractions

Materials   All fraction cards from 1 deck

- One student shuffles the cards and gives 5 cards to each student.
- The rest of the cards are placed fraction-side down in a pile.
- The goal is to find equivalent fractions.
- Student 1 says to one of the students, "Do you have a fraction equivalent to this fraction?" Student 1 then shows the fraction on the card.

- If the reply is "yes," that student must give the card to Student 1.
- If the answer is "no," Student 1 must go fishing and take a card from the deck.
- If Student 1 gets 2 equivalent fractions, either by asking or by "fishing," he or she places the cards on the table.
- The first student to run out of cards wins.

49 Activities

Greater Than

Object To make the 6-digit number with the greater value

Students 2

Skill Understanding place value; comparing whole numbers

Materials 1 deck for each student; paper; pencils

- Each student takes the 0–9 cards from his or her deck, shuffles them, and places them facedown.
- Each student takes 6 cards from the top of his or her deck and makes the greatest number possible.
- One student writes both numbers on a sheet of paper.
- Together students decide which number is greater and write a > or < to compare the numbers.
- Students repeat the activity by taking 6 more cards from their decks.

Try This

- Students make numbers with more or less than 6 digits.

 ## Integer Number Line

Object   To compare values of positive and negative numbers

Students   2 to 4

Skill   Comparing positive and negative numbers

Materials   Black cards 1–10, 1 of each; blue cards 0–10, 1 of each

---

- The black cards are positive integers and the blue cards are negative integers.
- Students arrange the cards to form a number line from –10 to 10.
- Students pose questions to each other. For example, "Which number is greater, –2 or –3?" or "Which number is less, 4 or –8?"

Try This

- Students ask each other questions, such as "What is the difference between –4 and 7?" The other students use the number line to answer the question.

51 Activities

Lucky Nine

Object To write a number sentence whose answer is as close to 9 as possible

Students 2 to 4

Skill Understanding the order of operations

Materials Paper; pencils

- One student shuffles the deck and gives 2 cards to each student. The rest of the cards are placed number-side down in a pile.
- Students make a number sentence using the 2 cards and any operation. The goal is to have a total that is as close to 9 as possible.
- Students may take one more card from the top of the deck. If a student takes a card, he or she must use it.
- Each student calculates the difference between the answer for her or his number sentence and 9. The difference is the student's score for that round.
- For example, a student receives a 2 card and a 3 card. The student takes another card, which is a 7. The student writes $7 + 3 - 2 = 8$. That student's score is 1 since $9 - 8 = 1$.
- The game is over when all cards have been used. The student with the lowest total wins.

◆ Match It

Object To get the greatest total

Skill Using equivalent names for numbers

Students 2 to 4

- The Dealer mixes the cards and gives 4 cards to each student. The Dealer also places 4 cards faceup on the table. The rest of the deck is placed number-side down in a pile.

- Students take turns. On a turn, the student looks for ways to combine the faceup cards so they match one card in his or her hand. For the number 5, the student could use a 5, or a 4 and a 1 to match it.

- The student takes the matching card(s) from the table and the card from his or her hand and puts them in a pile. The student replaces the faceup cards with cards from the deck and takes one card for his or her hand.

- If the student cannot make a match, the turn is over.

- The game is over when no more matches can be made. Each student adds the values of his or her cards. The student with the greatest total wins.

53 Activities

Matching Numbers with Counters

Object To select the number card that matches the counters

Students 2

Skill Connecting concrete representations to numerals

Materials 10 counters

- One student chooses any number of counters and places them on the table.
- The other student looks through the card deck to find a number card that matches the number of counters.
- Students then switch roles.

Take the Challenge

- Students use as many as 20 counters.

4 counters

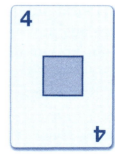
4 number card

 # Math Game

Object   To create a game

Students   1 or more

Skill   Understanding number theory, fractions, and operations

Materials   Paper; pencils

- Make up a game for one of these categories:
- Whole numbers: Use the number side of the cards. Your game can include odds and evens, primes and composites, square or triangular numbers.
- Fractions: Use the fraction side of the cards. Include anything you have learned about fractions, such as equivalent fractions, ordering fractions, or drawing pictures for fractions.

- Operations: Use either side of the cards. Include operations with whole numbers, fractions, or integers.
- You can work with another student.
- Your game could be similar to one you have already played.
- Write down the rules for your game.

Try This

- Trade your rules with another student and play his or her game.

55 Activities

Missing Addends

Object To find pairs of numbers that add up to 10

Students 2

Skill Thinking algebraically

Materials Two each of cards 1–10; paper; pencils; counters (for Try This)

- Each student takes one of each card 1 through 9, mixes them, and puts them number-side down in a pile.
- Each student takes a 10 card and puts it faceup next to his or her pile.
- Student 1 takes a card from his or her pile. Student 1 writes an addition problem with the card to answer the question: What number plus this number equals 10?
- Student 2 checks the work. If the problem is correct, then Student 2 takes a turn. If the problem is incorrect, then the students work together to correct it.

Try This

- Students may use counters to help them figure out how much they must add to each card to make 10.

Mixed Numbers

Object To form mixed numbers with the fraction cards

Students 2

Skill Recognizing the meaning of mixed numbers

- One student names a mixed number, such as $2\frac{1}{2}$.

- The other student finds the fraction cards that add up to that number. The student can use fractions that name whole numbers and combine them with simple fractions. For example, to make $2\frac{1}{2}$, the student can use the cards $\frac{3}{3}$, $\frac{4}{4}$, and $\frac{1}{2}$.

- Students switch roles.

$$\frac{3}{3} \quad + \quad \frac{4}{4} \quad + \quad \frac{1}{2} \quad = \quad 2\frac{1}{2}$$

57 Activities

Multiplication Top-It

Object To have the most cards at the end of the game

Students 2 to 4

Skill Practicing multiplication facts

- One student shuffles the cards and places the deck number-side down on the table.
- Each student turns over 2 cards and calls out the product of the numbers.
- The student with the greatest product wins the round and takes all the cards.
- If there is a tie, each tied student turns over 2 more cards and calls out their product. The student with the greatest product takes all the cards from both plays.
- Play ends when not enough cards are left for each student to have another turn. The student with the most cards wins.

 **Name That Number**

Object	To have the most cards at the end of the game	**Skill**	Using equivalent names for numbers
		Materials	Paper; pencils
Students	2 to 4		

- One student mixes the cards and places 5 cards number-side up on the table. The rest of the deck is placed facedown, and the top card is turned over. This is the "target number." Students take turns trying to name the target number by adding or subtracting the numbers on 2 of the 5 cards that are faceup.

- If a student can name the target number, he or she takes the 2 cards used to name it, along with the target-number card. All 3 cards are then replaced by drawing cards from the top of the deck.

- If a student cannot name the target number, the turn is over. The top card on the deck is turned over, and the number on this card becomes the new target number.

59 Activities

Name That Number (cont.)

- Play continues until all of the cards in the deck have been turned over. The student who has taken the most cards wins.

Take the Challenge

- Students try to name the target number by adding, subtracting, multiplying, or dividing the numbers on as many of the cards as possible.

 **Naming Figures**

Object To practice the names of geometric figures

Students 1 or more

Skill Identifying figures by numbers of sides

Materials 10 index cards; pencils and/or crayons

■ Write each of the following on a different index card:

line segment (1)   *hexagon (6)*

angle (2)   *heptagon (7)*

triangle (3)   *octagon (8)*

quadrangle or quadrilateral (4)   *nonagon (9)*

pentagon (5)   *decagon (10)*

■ Match cards that show figures to the words on the index cards. Discuss your reasons for each match.

Take the Challenge

■ Use the index cards and figure cards as flash cards. Can you name or draw each figure?

61 Activities

Number Guess

Object	To rename a number using any combination of operations, pictures, or words	**Skill**	Understanding the meaning of addition, subtraction, and multiplication
Students	2 or more	**Materials**	Index cards; pencils and/or crayons

- Student 1 mixes the cards and places them number-side down in a pile.
- Student 1 picks a card and hides it from the other students. He or she must write a different name for the number on an index card, using addition, subtraction, or multiplication. 5 could be renamed as 2 + 3 or 9 – 4.
- Student 1 shows his or her index card to the other students.
- The other students try to guess what the number on the hidden card is.
- The student who guesses the number first gets the next turn.
- If no one guesses the correct number, then Student 1 gets another turn.

Try This

- Students may also write words or draw pictures of the number using dots, lines, or other figures.

Number Line Game

Object	To be the first player to run out of cards	**Skill**	Understanding the meaning of positive and negative numbers
Students	2 to 4	**Materials**	All 0–5 cards or all 0–10 cards from 1 deck

- The Dealer shuffles the deck and gives 4 cards to each student.

- The Dealer puts 2 cards faceup on the table. These two cards make up part of a number line. The rest of the deck is placed facedown.

- Black numbers are positive and blue numbers are negative. Zero is neither positive nor negative, so the black and blue zeros are the same.

- Students take turns to complete the number line. They may put down cards 1 higher, 1 lower, or the same as the cards on the table.

- If a student cannot play a card, he or she must take one from the deck. If the card can be played, the student may put the card down right away. If the card cannot be played, the student keeps the card and the turn is over.

- The student who uses all his or her cards first wins the game.

63 Activities

Number Sentence Contest

Object To rename a number using different operations

Students 2 or more

Skill Writing number sentences for a given value

Materials Paper; pencils

- One student shuffles the cards and places them number-side down in a pile.
- Student 1 picks a card and shows it to the other students.
- Students use addition, subtraction, multiplication, and division to write as many number sentences as possible that rename the number on the card. Each number sentence must have only one operation.
- Students compare their number sentences.
- The student who has the most correct number sentences gets to pick the next card.

Take the Challenge

- Students may add new rules to each game, such as only subtraction can be used, or 3 numbers and 2 operations must be used.

Numbers and Dot Patterns I

Object   To copy a picture of dots with counters

Students   1

Skill   Connecting numerals with pictorial representations

Materials   10 counters

- Take the three 5 cards that have dots on them.
- Place them on the table in front of you.
- Use counters to make a design that matches the dots on the card.
- Do the same for other dot cards.

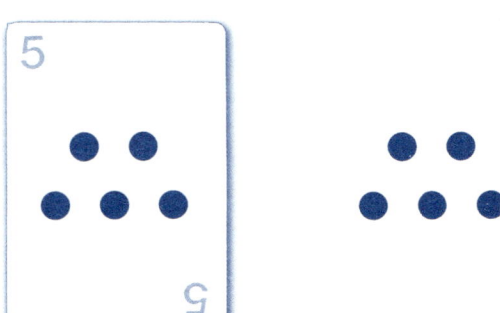

5 number
card with dots

A matching
dot pattern

65 Activities

Numbers and Dot Patterns II

Object To identify arrays, pictures of two addends, and geometric figures

Students 1 or more

Skill Classifying according to established criteria

■ Sort the cards into different groups:
- First find all the cards with dots arranged as a set of two addends, such as 4 + 5. Some cards can be thought of as the number plus zero, such as 5 + 0.
- Next find all the cards with dots shown in arrays. That is, the dots form squares, rectangles, or lines.
- Finally, find all the cards with geometric figures. For each of the geometric figure cards, try to find a dot card that goes with it. Explain your reasoning.

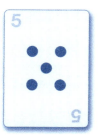

Odd and Even Numbers

Object   To identify odd and even numbers

Students   1

Skill   Counting by 2s

Materials   Paper; pencil

- Take out 1 card for each number from 1 to 20.
- Arrange the cards in order in a row.
- Move the 2 down to begin to form a second row.
- Begin at 2 and count by 2s. Pull down every number card you count into the second row.
- Which row shows odd numbers? Which row shows even numbers?

- Write down the next 5 odd numbers.
- Write down the next 5 even numbers.

Ordering a Set of Fractions

Object To order fractions from smallest to largest

Students 1 or more

Skill Ordering fractions

Materials Paper; pencils

- Take the following fraction cards from the deck: $\frac{4}{10}, \frac{1}{5}, \frac{6}{10}, \frac{3}{8}, \frac{3}{4}, \frac{7}{8}, \frac{8}{10}, \frac{5}{6}, \frac{2}{16}, \frac{5}{8}, \frac{2}{12}$.
- Put the cards in order from smallest to largest. You may use the blue shading on the cards to help you.
- Write the fractions from smallest to largest on the paper.

Take the Challenge

- Find a common denominator for $\frac{6}{10}$ and $\frac{5}{8}$. Which fraction is larger?
- Find a common denominator for $\frac{5}{6}$ and $\frac{8}{10}$. Which fraction is larger?

Ordering Fractions with Same Denominator

Object   To order fractions from least to greatest

Students   1 or more

Skill   Understanding fractions

- Find all the fraction cards in the deck that have the same number in the bottom of the fraction, the denominator. For example, find all the cards with "5" as the denominator.

- Put the cards in order from smallest to largest. Use the shaded parts of the cards to help you.

- Count the total number of parts on each card. Compare this number to the denominator.

- Count the total number of shaded parts on each card. Compare this number to the top number of the fraction, the numerator.

- Look at the number line at the bottom of the card. How is the number line similar to the shaded parts of the card?

Try This

- Repeat this activity with other sets of fractions from the deck.

69 Activities

Ordering Numbers

Object To order numbers from smallest to largest and from largest to smallest

Skill Counting forward and backward

Students 1

- Take one of each card 0 to 20.
- Mix the cards.
- Place the cards in order, faceup on your desk, from smallest to largest.
- Mix the cards again.
- Place the cards in order, faceup on your desk, from largest to smallest.

Try This

- Use a different set of cards, such as one of each card from 5 to 16, or from 3 to 12. Place the cards in order from smallest to largest, and then from largest to smallest.

Polygons

Object   To collect the most cards at the end of the game

Students   2 to 4

Skill   Recognizing and naming polygons

- One student mixes the cards and places the deck number-side down in the middle of the table.

- Students take turns flipping over a card to make a second pile.

- As each card is turned over, students watch for a polygon card to appear.

- The first student to name the polygon correctly gets all of the cards in the second pile.

- The game ends when all the cards have been turned over. The student with the most cards at the end of the game wins.

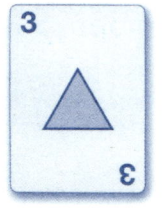
triangle

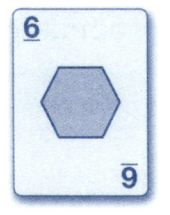
hexagon

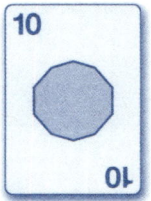
decagon

71 Activities

Polygons Alike and Different

Object To describe geometric figures

Students 2 or more

Skill Identifying properties of geometric figures

- Students sort out the cards with geometric figures.
- Students tell how the figures are alike and how they are different.
- Some students may use terms such as vertex, side, angle, interior, and exterior to describe these figures.
- Then students take turns asking each other to identify different figures. For example, "Show me a figure with 5 sides."

Take the Challenge

- Students find shapes in the classroom that match the ones on the cards.

 # Prime and Composite Facts

Object   To identify the factors of prime and composite numbers

Students   1

Skill   Identifying factors

Materials   Paper; pencil

- Take the cards that have dots arranged as lines, squares, or rectangles.

- Write as many multiplication facts as you can for each set of dots.

- Which dot cards have more than one multiplication fact?

2×5

10×1

Multiplication facts for 10, a composite number

Prime or Composite?

Object To arrange counters in specified patterns

Students 1

Skill Discovering properties of prime and composite numbers between 2 and 9

Materials 26 counters; paper; pencils

- Take the cards that have dots arranged as lines, squares, or rectangles.
- Place the 2, 3, 5, 7, and 9 cards on the table.
- Place 2 counters next to the 2 card, 3 counters next to the 3 card, and so on.
- Try to arrange each set of counters to form a square or a rectangle. Which group of counters makes a square? A rectangle?
- Identify which numbers are prime and which are composite.

Try This

- Sort all the dots cards into two piles. One pile is for composite numbers. The other pile is for prime numbers.

Primes and Composites

Object To arrange counters into square arrays

Students 1 or 2

Skill Discovering properties of prime and composite numbers between 11 and 20

Materials Cards 11–20 from 1 deck; paper; pencils; 20 counters

---

- Place the 11 card on the table in front of you.
- Take 11 counters and try to make a rectangular array with them.
- Try again using 12 counters, then 13 counters, and so on, up to 20.
- On your paper, keep track of which groups of counters can form a rectangular array and which cannot.
- Sort the cards into 2 piles: those whose counters form a rectangular array and those whose counters do not.
- Which group of cards shows prime numbers? Which group shows composite numbers?

Take the Challenge

- Without using counters, try to predict which numbers between 20 and 30 are prime.

Product Game

Object To get the highest score
Students 3

Skill Multiplying fractions
Materials All fraction cards from 1 deck; paper; pencils

- One student is the Dealer. The Dealer shuffles the deck and gives 3 cards fraction-side down to each of the other students.
- Each student turns his or her cards fraction-side up and chooses any 2 cards to multiply together.
- The student who gets a product closest to 1 wins the round and gets 1 point.
- The Dealer looks at each of the students' cards to see if a different set of cards would have made a product even closer to 1. If the Dealer finds a mistake, he or she wins 1 point.
- Students take turns being the Dealer after each round.
- The game is over when all the cards have been used. The student with the highest total score wins.

Product Production

Object	To make the greatest product	**Skill**	Multiplying a 2-digit number by a 1-digit number
Students	2 or more	**Materials**	All 0–9 cards from 1 deck; paper; pencils

- One student shuffles the cards and places them number-side down in a pile.

- Another student turns over 3 cards and places them on the table so everyone can see them.

- Each student works quickly to make up a 2-digit by 1-digit multiplication problem. The goal is to make the problem with the greatest product. Students may do their work on paper.

- Students share their results. The one who has the greatest product wins the round.

- One student turns over 3 new cards for the next round.

Try This

- Four cards are turned over. Students race to make a 2-digit by 2-digit problem, or a 3-digit by 1-digit problem.

77 Activities

Rectangular Arrays

Object To sort cards into primes and composites

Students 1

Skill Classifying numbers

Materials Cards 11–20; paper; pencil

- Use the cards numbered 11–20.
- Draw dot arrays for each of the numbers on the cards. Which group of dots can be arranged in a square array or rectangular array?
- After drawing the arrays, sort the cards into 2 piles: prime numbers and composite numbers. Which cards are in each pile?

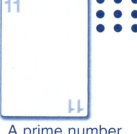

A prime number

A composite number

Smallest to Largest

Object To make 4-digit numbers and arrange them in order

Students 2 to 3

Skill Understanding place value

Materials All 0–9 cards from 1 deck

- One student shuffles the cards and gives 12 cards to each student.
- Each student uses his or her cards to make three 4-digit numbers.
- Each student arranges his or her numbers in order from smallest to largest.

Take the Challenge

- Students arrange all of their numbers from smallest to largest.

Sorting the Deck

Object   To classify dot designs by shape
Students   1
Skill   Recognizing shapes
Materials Paper; pencil

- Find all the cards that show dots.
- Sort the dot shapes into groups. Make a group for single dots, triangles, trapezoids, lines, squares, and rectangles.
- Draw pictures of other dot shapes using larger numbers.
- Decide in which group each of your pictures belongs.

Square Numbers

Object To identify square numbers

Students 2 to 4

Skill Developing visual thinking

Materials Paper; pencil; calculator (for Take the Challenge)

- Find all the cards in the deck that show dots that form a square. Include the 1 card.

- Put the cards in order from smallest to largest.

- Describe the patterns of cards and dots.

- Draw a square dot arrangement for 16.

Take the Challenge

- Use a calculator to find the square numbers up to 1,000.

81 Activities

Steps

Object To reach the other side of the room
Students 2 or more
Skill Recognizing number values
Materials 1 set of cards 0–10 per student

- Students line up along one side of the room with their backs to the wall.
- Each student mixes his or her cards and holds them in a pile, number-side down. Then each student turns over the top card.
- Dots on the card stand for "baby" steps. Figures on the card stand for "giant" steps.
- Each student takes the number of steps shown on his or her own card. A zero card means no steps are taken.
- Students continue turning over cards and taking steps across the room.
- As students reach the other side, they stand and wait for the rest of the students to finish.

Try This

- One student checks the other students' cards. Any student who takes the wrong number of steps is sent back to the starting wall.

Sums

Object To make the greatest sum possible

Students 2 or more

Skills Understanding place value and adding 4-digit numbers

- One student shuffles the deck and divides the cards evenly among all the students.

- Each student turns over 8 cards from his or her pile.

- Students arrange their cards to make two 4-digit numbers. Each student adds his or her two 4-digit numbers.

- The student with the greatest sum wins the round. Play continues until there are no more cards left.

Try This

- The goal of the activity can be changed to finding the greatest difference.

83 Activities

Top-It

Object To have the most cards at the end of the game

Skill Comparing whole numbers

Students 2

- One student mixes the cards and places them number-side down in a pile.
- Each student takes a card from the top of the deck, turns it over, and says the number on the card.
- The student who has the larger number takes both cards. If the 2 cards show the same number, each student takes another card from the top of the deck. The student with the larger number takes all 4 cards.
- The game is over when all the cards have been taken. The student with more cards wins.

Try This

- Students can determine who wins at the end of the game by flipping a penny.

  Heads: The student with more cards wins.

  Tails: The student with fewer cards wins.

Top-It with Integers

Object   To have the most cards at the end of the game

Students   2 to 4

Skill   Adding and subtracting integers

- One student shuffles the cards and places the deck number-side down.

- The black numbers are positive. The blue numbers are negative. Remember that zero is neither positive nor negative, so the black zero and blue zero are the same.

- Each student turns over 2 cards and calls out their sum. The student with the highest sum takes all the cards. If necessary, students can check answers with a calculator.

For example:
- Student 1 turns over a blue 5 and a black 7. $-5 + 7 = 2$
- Student 2 turns over a blue 3 and a blue 4. $-3 + (-4) = -7$
- Student 1 takes all 4 cards because 2 is greater than -7.

- In case of a tie, each tied student turns over 2 more cards and calls out the sum. The student with the highest sum takes all the cards from both plays.

Top-It with Integers (cont.)

- Play continues until there are too few cards left for each student to have another turn. The student who took the most cards wins.

Try This

- Play the game with subtraction. Each student turns over 2 cards, one at a time, and subtracts the second number from the first number. The student with the greatest difference takes all the cards.

Example:
- Student 1 turns over a black 2 first, and then a blue 3.
  $+2 - (-3) = 5$
- Student 2 turns over a blue 5 first, and then a black 8.
  $-5 - (+8) = -13$
- Student 1 takes all 4 cards because 5 is greater than -13.

Triangular Numbers

Object   To discover the pattern for triangular numbers

Child   1 or more

Skill   Developing visual thinking

Materials   50 counters; paper; pencils

- Find all the cards in the deck that show dots that form a triangle. Include the 1 card.
- Put the cards in order from smallest to largest.
- Use counters to make each triangle.
- Use the counters to form the next 5 triangular numbers.

Take the Challenge

- Write the number patterns for the next 5 triangular numbers.

Triple Challenge

Object To have the most cards at the end of the game

Students 2

Skill Writing expressions to make the smallest whole number possible

Materials Paper; pencils

- One student shuffles the deck and divides the cards evenly between the 2 students.
- Each student turns over 3 cards. Students try to make the smallest possible whole number with those 3 numbers, using any combination of operations.
- The student with the smaller whole number wins all the cards. For example:
  - A student with cards 1, 2, and 9 writes $9 \div (2 + 1) = 3$.
  - The other student with cards 4, 2, and 1 writes $4 - 2 - 1 = 1$.
  - The second student wins all the cards.

  If there is a tie, the student whose cards have the smaller sum wins and takes all the cards.
- The game is over when all the cards in the deck have been used. The student with more cards wins.

 # Unit Fractions

Object   To identify all fractions with 1 as the numerator

Students   1

Skill   Recognizing the parts and meaning of fractions

■ Take out all the fraction cards that have a 1 as the top number of the fraction (the numerator). These are called unit fractions.

■ Put the cards in order from smallest fraction to largest fraction.

■ Make observations about the fractions:

- How much is shaded on each fraction card?

- How many parts is the card divided into? How does this number relate to the parts on the number line?

- How does the bottom number of the fraction (the denominator) relate to the number of parts on the card and on the number line?

- What statement can you make about the denominator and the size of the parts on the card?

89 Activities

Writing 1 as a Fraction

Object To find fractions that represent 1

Students 1

Skill Finding equivalent names for numbers

- Pull out all the fraction cards that are shaded completely.
- What do you notice about these cards?
- What do you notice about the number line at the bottom of each card?
- What do you notice about the fraction that describes the card?

Take the Challenge

- Write or draw any 5 fractions, other than the ones on the cards, that are equivalent to 1.

$\frac{5}{5}$ $\frac{4}{4}$ $\frac{2}{2}$